GRADE

6

GU01017992

The Syllabus of Examinations shou requirements, especially those for sight-reading. Attention should k Notices on the inside front cover, w any changes.

The syllabus is obtainable from music retailers or from The Associated Board of the Royal Schools of Music, 24 Portland Place, London W1B 1LU, United Kingdom (please send a stamped addressed C5 (162mm x 229mm) envelope).

In examination centres outside the UK, information and syllabuses may be obtained from the Local Representative.

CONTENTS

Where appropriate, pieces in this volume have been checked with original source material and edited as necessary for instructional purposes. Any editorial additions to the texts are given in small print, within square brackets, or – in the case of slurs and ties – in the form ⌢. Fingering, phrasing, pedalling, metronome marks and the editorial realization of ornaments (where given) are for guidance only; they are not comprehensive or obligatory.

Editor for the Associated Board: **Richard Jones**

DO NOT
PHOTOCOPY
© MUSIC

Alternative pieces for this grade

Music origination by Barnes Music Engraving Ltd.
Cover by Økvik Design.
Printed in England by Headley Brothers Ltd,
The Invicta Press, Ashford, Kent.

Allegro

Fourth movement from Sonata No. 8 in C

PESCETTI

Allegro [♩ = c.96]

Giovanni Battista Pescetti (c.1704 –66) was an Italian musician who found employment in Venice and London, chiefly as a composer of operas but also as a harpsichord player. In this Allegro quavers might be lightly detached. Dynamics are left to the player's discretion.
Source: *Sonate per gravicembalo* (London, 1739)

Invention No. 15 in B minor

BWV 786

J. S. BACH

The 15 Inventions in two contrapuntal parts, BWV 772–86, were originally written for the musical education of Bach's eldest son, Wilhelm Friedemann. According to the composer, they were designed to foster a 'cantabile style of playing'. Dynamics are left to the player's discretion. Quavers might be lightly detached, except those of the thematic falling 2nd (b. 1, RH, third crotchet etc.), which, as an appoggiatura figure, should be slurred.

Source: autograph MS, Staatsbibliothek zu Berlin, Preussischer Kulturbesitz, Mus. ms. Bach P 610

Reproduced from J. S. Bach: *Inventions & Sinfonias*, BWV 772–801, edited by Richard Jones (Associated Board)

A:3

Andante amoroso

Second movement from Sonata in B flat, K. 281/189f

MOZART

K. 281, from which this slow movement is drawn, is one of Mozart's earliest piano sonatas, written during a visit to Munich in early 1775 when he was just 19 years old. Denis Matthews invites us to imagine the opening melody in thirds as if played on clarinets, and remarks that 'the epithet "amoroso" points to a special mood, tender rather than passionate'. Mozart's characteristic staccato wedge over a tied note in b. 68 presumably implies that this note should be given the same attack as the previous four notes.
Source: autograph MS, formerly in Preussische Staatsbibliothek, Berlin

Adapted from Mozart: *Sonatas for Pianoforte*, Vol. I, edited by Stanley Sadie and Denis Matthews (Associated Board)

B:1

Tango

No. 2 from *España*, Op. 165

ALBÉNIZ

The Spanish composer and pianist Isaac Albéniz (1860–1909) travelled widely in Europe and America; he formed close ties with, among others, d'Indy, Dukas and Fauré. His piano works absorb the idioms of Spanish folk-dance music. The tango, however, probably originated in Buenos Aires. In b. 36 the rhythm of the top part is to be assimilated to the triplets of the middle part, as shown by the alignment.
Source: *España: 6 Feuilles d'Album*, Op. 165 (London, 1890)

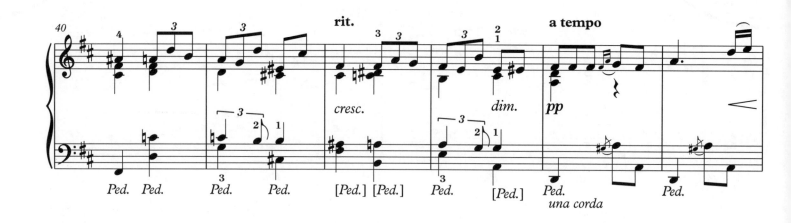

Nuances

No. 3 from *Quatre morceaux*, Op. 56

B:2

Edited by
Howard Ferguson

SKRYABIN

Aleksandr Nikolayevich Skryabin (1872–1915) was not only a composer but a brilliant concert pianist, who performed chiefly his own music. He wrote in a very personal and highly chromatic post-Wagnerian style.
Source: *Quatre morceaux pour piano*, Op. 56 (Leipzig: M. P. Belaieff, 1908)

Curiose Geschichte

No. 2 from *Kinderscenen*, Op. 15

SCHUMANN

Schumann wrote *Scenes from Childhood* Op. 15, from which this piece, 'Strange Story', is drawn, shortly after his engagement to Clara Wieck and in the midst of a five-year period when he was concentrating exclusively on piano music. The metronome mark is Schumann's, though it should be noted that Clara, in her collected edition of his works, gave ♩ = 132. Players should decide for themselves which to adopt. The grace notes in b. 1 and parallel places are to be played before the beat. Discreet use of the sustaining pedal is recommended throughout.
Source: *Kinderscenen: Leichte Stücke für das Pianoforte*, Op. 15 (Leipzig: Breitkopf & Härtel, 1839)

Adapted from Schumann: *Kinderscenen*, Op. 15, edited by Howard Ferguson (Associated Board)

C:1

Reverie

CHICK COREA

Slowly, quasi-rubato ♩ = 52

The composer describes this piece thus: 'Wistful introspection; a tear'. Pedalling is left to the player's discretion, but note that its use is essential for sustaining many of the LH chords.

ADO Universal Studios. Universal/MCA Music Publishing Ltd, Elsinore House, 77 Fulham Palace Road, London W6 8JA. Used by permission of Music Sales Ltd. All Rights Reserved. International Copyright Secured. All enquiries for this piece apart from the examinations should be addressed to Music Sales Ltd, 8/9 Frith Street, London W1D 3JB.

Pedal.

Columbine Dances

No. 1 from *Puppets*, Vol. 1

MARTINŮ

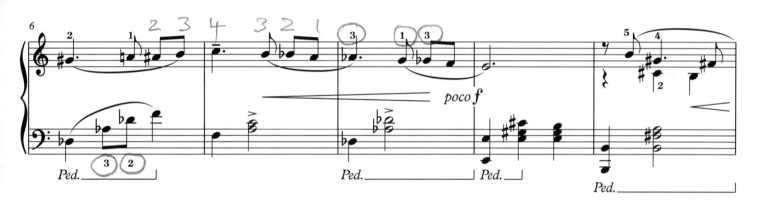

The Czech composer Bohuslav Martinů (1890–1959) was extremely prolific in all branches of composition, including piano music, despite the fact that he began his career as a violinist rather than a composer. His music often shows the influence of Czech folk music.

AB 2831

Yellow Beanleaves

JULIAN YU

The composer has written: 'This piece reflects the percussive quality and noisy, jubilant atmosphere of northern Chinese wind and percussion folk music, which was often played at weddings and other large gatherings. One such traditional piece is called *Yellow Beanleaves*, from which my work takes its title.' The piece was completed in Melbourne on 6 December 1999. Note that the pedal is needed to sustain the LH chord in bb. 10–11.

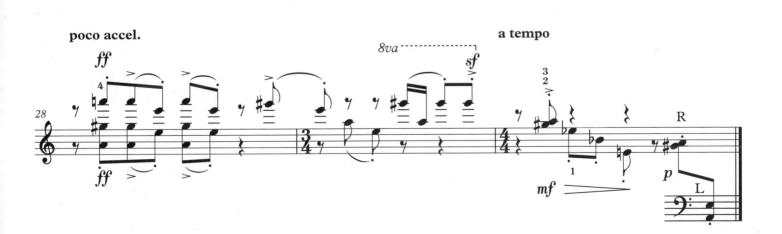